D0725413

OFF THE WALL

EGYPTIAN ART

Ruthie Knapp and Janice Lehmberg

Davis Publications, Inc.
Worcester, Massachusetts

Hello! I'm your tour guide, Rembrandt. This is a painting I did of myself. I have done lots of portraits of myself—about 100, in fact. In 1629 I finished this painting called *Artist in His Studio*. And *I'm* the artist, Rembrandt.

I've spent almost four hundred years trying to finish the painting on the easel. Do I ever need a break!

I am going to hang up my palette with the one you see behind me on the wall and unlatch the door to your right. Then I can join you from time to time as you read this book. I would like to help you look at Egyptian art. After all, three centuries of painting have taught me a trick or two!

Rembrandt van Rijn, *Artist in His Studio,* 1629.

© 1998 Janice G. Lehmberg and Ruth C. Knapp
Illustrations © John McIntosh of McIntosh Ink, Inc.

Printed in Italy
Library of Congress Catalog Number 98-60874
ISBN: 0-87192-384-X
10 9 8 7 6 5 4 3 2 1

Front cover: Gold Death Mask of Tutankhamun. Photo courtesy Fred J. Maroon. ©Maroon Photography, Inc., Washington, DC.

A contribution from the proceeds of the sale of this book will be donated to The Sally Leahy Scholarship Fund. Scholarships are awarded to children from the Greater Boston area for art classes held at the Museum of Fine Arts.

Contents

INTRODUCTION

Museum is a word like eggplant. It doesn't sound appealing. Children and adults often don't want to go to museums. How many times have you or a friend gone to museum in anticipation of a stimulating experience? It sounds easy enough: centuries of culture will speak to you from age-darkened canvases, sculptures, and small coins. History will come clear. Well, if history doesn't come clear, at least you'll be surrounded by many beautiful old things. Wrong!

Welcome to museum feet

"Museum feet" is that tired feeling you get after spending too much time in a museum. A case of museum feet makes you feel like saying: "This is boring. I could have done that myself. That's ugly. I'm hungry. I'm really hot. When can we sit down? What time is it?"

Studies of museum behavior show that the average visitor spends four seconds looking at an object. Children are more interested in smells, sounds, the "feel" of a place, and other people's faces than they are in looking at a work of art. Adults, sometimes unfamiliar with what they are seeing, cannot always answer children's questions. After a museum visit, it is only a short time before most everything is forgotten. Within a family or group of five, no one member will remember a shared looking experience the same way.

We have written this book to help people of all ages enjoy new ways of looking at works of art, ways that make looking memorable and fun. Come with us and learn how to banish the **boring** and feature the **fun.**

? **Why do museums show so much old stuff?** Not all museums collect old things. There are hundreds of different kinds of museums in the United States. They range from a nut museum, to a Mack truck museum, to the biggest thermometer museum. There is even a museum of bad art!

Symbols to Help You Read This Book

Use your flashlight

Common questions

A good idea

Look closely at museum objects

Additional information

Avoiding Museum Feet

To avoid museum feet, try not to look at too many things. Studies show that young visitors get more out of a visit if they focus on seven (plus or minus two) objects—either five or nine objects. The fewer objects you see, the more you'll remember. One and a half hours is the ideal time to keep your eyes and mind sharp, and your feet happy!

Making personal connections with museum objects helps to form lasting memories. For example, if you are looking at a sculpture of an Egyptian Pharaoh, you can relate the distant past to the present by saying, "Who would take the place of a Pharaoh today?"

"You can enjoy a work of art for as long as it takes to smell an orange. Then to keep your interest you have to do something more."
— SIR KENNETH CLARK,
BRITISH ART HISTORIAN, 1903–1983

This book is about doing something more.

What to bring
✓ Paper and pencil with eraser
✓ Sit-on-the-floor clothes
✓ A plan of action
✓ A small flashlight
✓ A snack for the ride

Finding Your Way

A museum may feel big and confusing when you first arrive. If you are not familiar with the museum, find the Information Center or a guard. Ask for directions to the collection you want to see. Rooms in a museum are called **galleries.**

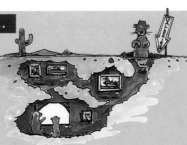

Museums are not the only places that have galleries. Prairie dogs, moles, and ants live in underground galleries. Old ships had galleries and so did forts.

What do BC and AD mean after dates? In 532 AD, a monk named Dennis the Short came up with a system to date events in history. He chose the year he believed Christ was born and called it 1 AD. AD stands for *anno domini* which is Latin for "in the year of our Lord." Everything that happened after Christ's birth is identified by the letters AD. Events that occurred before Christ's birth are identified by the letters BC, which stand for "before Christ." The year 50 BC is farther away in time than 10 BC.

Instruments/thingamabobs in museum galleries and cases

Some visitors are as interested in conservation equipment as they are in the objects on display. The *hygrometer* is a small dial that measures the humidity inside a display case. The *hygrothermograph* is a larger device that records the temperature and humidity of a museum gallery. These are often seen on the floor in a corner of the gallery. *Silica gel* is used to control the humidity in exhibit cases.

Why can't we touch things? Fingers contain oils and salts which hurt fragile museum objects. Have you ever seen the mark your fingerprint leaves on a blackboard?

Labels

Every work of art in a museum has a label. In an Egyptian collection, a label might look like this:

Name of art —— **Mummy with portrait panel**
Location —— **from Nile Delta**
Date of art —— **Roman period, 30 BC – 30 AD**
Medium —— **Wax on wood panel with linen bandages**
Acquisition information —— **Gift of Fay Rose Land** 1985.11

Accession number

Let's look at the label above. You are looking at a mummy with its portrait painted on a wooden panel. It was found in the delta of the Nile River, and it was made sometime during the Roman period. The mummy is wrapped in linen strips, and its portrait is painted with wax on a wood panel. Fay Rose Land gave the mummy to the museum. The person who was mummified lived sometime during the period thirty years before the birth of Christ to thirty years after his birth. Wow! That means it could be more than 2,000 years old!

Accession numbers The accession number on the label is 1985.11, which means the museum acquired the mummy in 1985. It was the eleventh object to be collected that year. You sometimes see small red numbers painted on the back and sides of small objects in a museum. These are also accession numbers.

Your Turn to Smell the Orange

Now it is your turn to smell the orange; otherwise known as getting your first impression. Choose an object. Let your eyes wander all over the surface. Absorb it. It is special, and it is yours. If you are looking at an Egyptian sculpture, walk all around it if you can. Look at it face to face, from its side and its back. Squat down and look up. Taking time to look at a work of art is important because there is always more to it than first meets the eye.

Study the drawing carefully. What is it? Ask someone else what he or she thinks it is. Once you have taken a long look at a work of art, turn away from it. Wait a few seconds and turn back to look at it again. What is *new* this time?

Look at Color

Colors can make us feel a certain way. They send messages. There are warm and cool colors. Warm colors are reds, oranges, and yellows. They might make us think of fire. Restaurant owners often use red in their decor because it can make people feel hungry. Cool colors are blues, greens, and violets. They might make us think of glaciers and ice. Rooms in hot climates are often painted blue to look cool and fresh.

Think about what different colors mean to you. Is yellow a cheerful color? Does it make you think of sunshine or a sizzling egg, sunny-side up? Vincent van Gogh, the Dutch artist, said that for him yellow was the color of love. Does black seem scary or sad? Does it bring to mind being alone in a dark house at night? Endless space? Does green remind you of your classroom walls?

Nature's paint box Egyptian artworks carved in stone were normally painted, but over time, colors have faded or worn away. Craftspeople used colors derived from ground-up minerals and plants. White came from chalk. Black came from charcoal and cooking pot bottoms. Iron oxides made reds, and

yellow ochre clay made yellow. Craftspeople painted sculptures with rushes and frayed twig brushes.

Sphinx of Amenhotep II. The brilliant turquoise color of this sculpture comes from a paste made of crushed quartz and copper oxide

Look at Shape

Shapes, like colors, can send messages to museum viewers. The oval is a shape often seen in Egyptian art. The Pharaoh's name was indicated by a cartouche, an oval shape with hieroglyphs inside. The symbol for a scarab beetle is also oval.

Sphinx of Ramses II. Most sculptures of Pharaohs have carved cartouches on the base, indicating who is represented.

Only a royal name can be placed inside a cartouche. The cartouche represents a circle of rope and implies that the Pharaoh's power surrounds everything on earth. Look for an oval shape filled with hieroglyphs in your gallery.

Cartouche of Sesotris I.

Coffins and tomb doors are rectangles. Stand in front of any sculpture. Making a straight line in the air with your finger, connect the left shoulder of a figure with its right shoulder. Bring the line down to the right corner of the base on which the figure sits or stands. Connect it to the left base corner. Draw the line up to the left shoulder. What shape have you traced in the air? Most Egyptian sculptures were carved from large, rectangular blocks of stone. When looking at portrait sculptures, you can usually detect the shape of the original square block.

The biggest triangles in Egyptian art are, of course, the pyramids.

Hatshepsut.

You will also notice circles in Egyptian art. Look for a sun disk on the sun god's head and in hieroglyphs. Look for round knobs in people's hands.

Word Wizard

Hieroglyphs Long ago, Greek travelers in Egypt saw strange symbols and pictures carved on Egyptian temples. They called these symbols the Greek words for *sacred* (hieros) and *carving* (glyphein). Hieroglyphs were used as written language in ancient Egypt.

Look at Line

Lines may be diagonal, curved, vertical, or horizontal. Diagonal lines are action lines. Curved lines also lend a sense of motion. A vertical line is a strong, stable line. It gives a feeling of balance. A horizontal line is a quiet line.

Word Wizard

Horizontal The word *horizontal* comes from *horizon,* the seemingly flat line where earth meets sky.

Figures in Egyptian art are usually seated or standing. Their bodies are rigid and vertical. The arms of standing figures hang close to their sides and are often pointing straight down to the ground. Their legs are straight. An Egyptian sculpture had to be strong and stable to house the spirit of the deceased forever. Its vertical lines lend an enduring air.

Look at Composition

The way an artist arranges the color, line, and shape in a work of art is called *composition.* When you decorate a birthday cake or doodle on a frosty windowpane, you are making a composition. Artists plan their compositions to guide our eyes on a journey through their artwork.

Egyptian artists arranged their paintings and relief carvings for tomb walls and coffins in horizontal zones or registers. Placing figures this way makes them easy to see and understand. These surface decorations were painted or carved as flat shapes with no shading or background.

Look at Sculpture

A sculpture is an object that can be measured three ways. It has length, width, and thickness or a front, a back, and sides—three dimensions. Since earliest times, people have made sculptures out of clay, bone, wood, and stone. Some sculptures are created by *carving away* material, like a pumpkin. In others, you *add* materials as you do when you make a snowman or a drip sandcastle. They can be huge like the Sphinx or tiny like a Stone Age arrowhead.

Most of the Egyptian sculpture you will see is made of stone. Egypt had abundant rock quarries near the Nile River and in the desert. Sandstone and limestone were the usual building stones. The much harder red and black granite and alabaster were commonly used in portrait sculpture. Egyptian sculpture is often broken and chipped because it is thousands of years old.

Egypt's native timber was of poor quality for large objects, but the Egyptians used it for domestic utensils and furniture. They used imported timber for large building projects.

Lion statuette.

To help you look at a sculpture, use the letters of the verb **SCULPT**.

S Surface, Scale, and Space Is the surface the same everywhere? Is the scale life-size? How much space do you need to look at the sculpture?

C Condition Is the piece all there? Has weather aged it? Are pieces missing? Has it been fixed or restored?

U Unlike If it is human, how is the sculpture **unlike** me? If it is an animal, how is it unlike the real animal?

L Light Is the sculpture the same color all over? Where is it darkest? Do the gallery lights make some parts appear darker or did the artist intend them to be darker?

P Placement Did the sculptor make this sculpture for a particular place?

T Touch, Texture, Title If you could touch this sculpture, how would it feel? smooth? cold? bumpy? What material is it made of? What textures do you notice? What title did the sculptor give this piece? What title would you give it?

ARCHAEOLOGY

The word **archaeology** comes from two Greek words: *archaia* meaning "old" and *logos* meaning "science." Archaeology is the study of old things. Archaeologists are detectives. Each object they find is a clue to how people lived thousands of years ago. Almost everything we know about ancient Egypt is a result of the work of archaeologists.

Can you think of other words that end in *-ology*? Zoology is the study of animals. Gemology is the study of precious stones or gems. What is mythology?

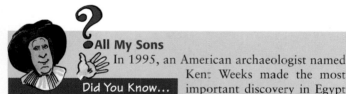

All My Sons

Did You Know... In 1995, an American archaeologist named Kent Weeks made the most important discovery in Egypt since King Tutankhamun's tomb was opened in 1922. After nine years spent working on the Valley of the Kings, Weeks unearthed sixty-seven burial chambers belonging to the sons of Egypt's greatest Pharaoh, King Ramses II (1301–1234 BC). It is believed that Ramses fathered more than one hundred children! Although scholars think that he fathered fifty daughters, their remains have not been found. Weeks says he expects to spend the rest of his life excavating the site.

Some children decide at an early age that they want to be archaeologists. Sir Flinders Petrie, the father of Egyptian archaeology, made up his mind when he was six years old. Kent Weeks knew he wanted to become an archaeologist by the time he was nine.

Have kids made amazing discoveries? You bet! Children have made awesome archaeological discoveries. In England in 1858, a young boy and his dog discovered a hoard of silver that had been buried by Vikings. In 1940, four French boys found prehistoric wall paintings in caves at Lascaux. More recently, a Bedouin shepherd boy hunting for a missing sheep threw a stone into a cave by the Dead Sea (Israel). He heard the sound of smashing pots. By chance, he had discovered jars containing the Dead Sea Scrolls, one of the most important finds in history!

ART S COOP

Hats off! An American, a German, and an Italian archaeologist were each given rights to dig at the three pyramids at Giza in 1902. How did they decide who got the small, medium, and large pyramid? Paper strips were drawn out of a hat belonging to the wife of one of the archaeologists. The American archaeologist drew rights to excavate the smallest pyramid. He hoped tomb robbers had paid less attention to the smallest pyramid. They had!

The three pyramids at Giza. The three pyramids can be seen beyond the flooded Nile River.

Years ago, people could take archaeological remains from foreign countries. Records were not kept. The sculptured friezes from the Greek Parthenon, now in the British Museum, were taken to England in 1806. Many objects in museums today were brought back by travelers and collectors before it was against the law.

Today, an archaeologist must receive a contract to dig in a foreign country. Every object that is discovered belongs to the country where it is found. The local government gets first pick from the dig and decides what the archaeologist may keep.

Archaeologist in pit.

A Closer Look

Look at groupings of artifacts in an Egyptian collection: pots, flint blades, and jewelry. Notice how they are mounted and displayed. You might start a collection of finds from your own yard or a friend's—coins, shells, interesting pebbles, and marbles, to name a few.

How do things get buried? Leaves, animals, dust in the atmosphere, sand, construction, and earthworms can help cover things up. Earthworms cause particular problems for archaeologists because they mix up layers of soil used in dating. This disturbance of the soil is called **bioturbation.**

Word Wizard

Artifact The word *artifact* is an archaeological term for something dug up. It comes from the Latin, *arte*, meaning "art," and *factum*, meaning "something made."

MUMMIES

The ancient Egyptians believed that each person was born with a twin spirit called a *ka.* Neither one could survive without the other. A person who died could live on in the afterlife only if his or her *ka* had food and a mummy to live in. That is why the Egyptians went to such pains to make everlasting mummies.

What is a mummy? In Egyptian collections, mummies are a deadly attraction! Seriously though, a mummy is a carefully preserved dead person, usually wrapped in linen.

Why is it called a mummy? Does it have children? Mummies have nothing to do with moms. Men, women, children, cats, dogs, birds, mice, and even crocodiles were mummified in ancient Egypt. The word *mummy* comes from the Arabic word *mummiya,* which describes a sticky, blackish tar-like substance called bitumen. Visitors to ancient Egypt mistakenly thought the dark resin covering mummies and in their linen wrappings was bitumen.

Is there really somebody in there? Yes! But today you don't have to unwrap mummies to prove it. A CT scan, a kind of X-ray that shows a slice-by-slice cross-section of the human body (picture a loaf of sliced bread), can tell us about the mummy's teeth, gums, arteries, bones, and tumors—even its sinuses! A CT scan can also tell if the person had diseases such as arthritis or tuberculosis. X-rays show if the mummy is wearing jewelry and if good luck charms, such as scarabs, were tucked into the many layers of linen wrapping.

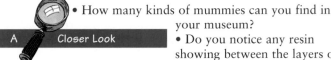

A   Closer Look

• How many kinds of mummies can you find in your museum?
• Do you notice any resin showing between the layers of linen?

Security Under Wraps

The clay scarab represents a scarab beetle, which was believed to be a form of the sun god. This beetle is part of the dung beetle family that rolls a small ball of manure between its back legs. It lays eggs in a ball of manure, which the baby beetles eat after they hatch. This odd habit made this beetle a symbol of renewed life. Amulets in the form of scarab beetles were commonly used to protect a mummy in its tomb.

ART SCOOP

Call the ambulance! One museum sent some of its mummies to be CT scanned at a local hospital. An ambulance picked up these elderly patients to take them to their doctor's appointment!

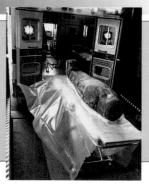

Mummies entering an ambulance.

How come the mummy looks so small? The body shrank during the mummy-making process. After death, a person's body was prepared for a trip to an afterlife of" millions and millions of years." The intestines, liver, lungs, and stomach were removed and put in containers called **canopic** (pronounced *ken*-oh-pick) **jars**. The brain was thrown away. The heart was left in place because it had to be weighed on the Scales of Truth in the afterlife. (In later years, the heart was removed, and a scarab was put in its place.) A salt called *natron* was put both inside and outside the body. The body was then left to dry in the sun for many weeks. The desert heat and salt crystals removed all moisture. You might compare a mummy's shrinking to a grape drying into a raisin.

Canopic jars with Cynocephalous head. The four sons of the falcon god, Horus, protected a mummy's insides. They are human, jackal, hawk, and baboon.

Feeling ill? The mnemonic **I L L S** will help you remember which parts of the body were removed to make a mummy.

I = intestines
L = liver
L = lungs
S = stomach

Mummy of Ramses II.

? **What does a mummy's body look like now?** It's just skin and bones. The skin looks like belt leather, dried fish, and rawhide strips wrapped around a skeleton!

? **What happened after the body dried out?** It was packed with a stuffing, like sawdust, and covered with a coat of resin (sap from a tree or plant). Then it was wrapped in many layers of linen. Sometimes good luck charms were slipped into the wrappings. Then a priest performed a ceremony called the "opening of the mouth." A magic wand was touched to the mouth, eyes, and other parts of the mummy. It was believed that these motions would allow the dead person to eat, speak, see, and walk in the afterlife.

Did You Know...

The human body is about ⅔ water!

REST IN PEACE The headrest magically kept the mummy's head from getting separated from its body. No one is sure how headrests were used. People probably lay on their sides and used pillows to make it comfortable.

Ah-choo! The nose of Ramses's mummy was packed with pepper-corns to preserve its distinct shape!

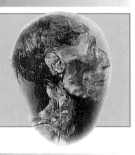

Head of Ramses II. Although the head of Ramses II is more than 3,000 years old, the teeth, hair, and skin are still well preserved.

Shabtis

The word *shabti* means "answerers." Shabtis are small figurines shaped like mummies. They were buried with mummies, and their purpose was to serve a mummy in the afterlife. Ancient Egyptians believed they could order shabtis to do unpleasant tasks for them. Some shabtis are inscribed with the words, "Here I am. How can I help?" Some mummies had a shabti for every day of the year. One Pharaoh had more than two thousand shabtis in his tomb to serve him in the afterlife.

Shabti of Sati. This shabti is holding two baskets and farming tools, a hoe, and a pick. It was made for a woman named Sati.

A Closer Look

- Look for a shabti figure in your gallery.
- Is it holding work tools in its hands?

What was the afterlife? The afterlife was the kingdom of the dead ruled by the Egyptian god, Osiris. The ancient Egyptians imagined it to be a happy place, similar to Egypt.

This case was custom fit for a mummy. It was made of linen or papyrus soaked in plaster which was wrapped around a clay dummy. After it hardened, the case was painted and the clay dummy was removed. Then the real mummy was put into an opening in the back. This case is painted with symbols of Osiris, the god of the afterlife, and his wife Isis, goddess of magic. They protect Nespanetjerenpere, who was a priest, on his journey to the afterlife.

Mummy cartonnage of Nespanetjerenpere.

Isis was a protector goddess in funeral rites and is sometimes shown on coffins with outspread wings. She had great magical powers.

Anubis was the god of the cemetery and mummification. He is usually shown with the head of a jackal and can often be seen on the outside of coffins. The Egyptians hoped that Anubis would prepare them for the afterlife. They believed that he weighed the heart of every person and told the mummy, "You will live forever."

Statuette of the god Anubis.

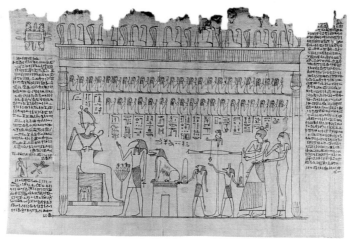

The Book of the Dead of Nes-Min. Notice the monster Ammit waiting to eat up the mummy as its heart is weighed.

But First, a Dangerous Journey...

As the mummy passed from one world to another, it had to overcome obstacles. It had to pass fierce gate gods with names like Secret Listener and Face Eraser. Then it had to shake off prowling cavern gods who had catfish heads and lived off corpses. Scarier still was the grisly baboon god who killed on sight. Finally, the mummy had to face questions from forty-two demons in the Hall of Two Truths. There its heart was weighed against the "feather of truth." If its heart balanced with the feather of truth, the mummy could go to the afterlife. But if its heart was heavy with sin, the mummy would be eaten by Ammit, a monster-mix of hippopotamus, crocodile, and lion.

Ammit was shown as a beast of land and water, suggesting that there was no escape for sinners.

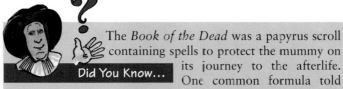

Did You Know...

The *Book of the Dead* was a papyrus scroll containing spells to protect the mummy on its journey to the afterlife. One common formula told the mummy how to disguise itself by changing into another form. A copy of the *Book of the Dead* was buried with mummies during one period in ancient Egypt. Some copies were known to have been as long as 100 feet.

• In the Egyptian collection you are visiting, look for Thoth in a scene from the *Book of the Dead*. He has the head of an ibis and the body of a man. He records the weighing of the heart.
• Can you find the feather of truth and the mummy's heart in a jug on hanging scales?

Thoth was the god of wisdom, writing, and the moon. He took the form of either a wading bird with a long bill called an ibis, or a baboon. His crown shows a crescent moon supporting the full moon. Thoth was also the god of scribes.

Would I be a mummy if I lived back then? Yes, if you or your family had the means to pay the mummy makers! But not everyone could afford such time-consuming burials. Preparing a mummy could take more than two months. The mummies of wealthy people were placed in tombs or fancy coffins and hidden in carved-out niches of rocky cliffs. Poor people were wrapped in woven mats and laid in shallow graves in the sand.

Burial pit.

Herodotus Much of what we know about mummies is because of a Greek historian named Herodotus. He traveled to Egypt in the fifth century BC and wrote detailed accounts of how mummies were made. Herodotus has been called "the father of history."

Art Oops! Loco-mummies

In the 19th century, mummies were used in surprising ways. While the Egyptians burned them as locomotive fuel, an American paper manufacturer turned linen mummy wrappings into brown paper. Around 1900, England ordered a shipment of 300,000 cat mummies to use for fertilizer. At that time, some people paid to attend exhibitions where mummies were unwrapped and dissected by surgeons.

What have mummies taught us? The X-rays of sixty mummies in 1998 revealed a lot about the life of the ordinary Egyptian family. They show there was a high death rate during childbirth for both the mother and baby. Life expectancy was about thirty-eight years, and if you lived to be fifty you were really ancient! Finally, the X-rays showed bone deformities and arthritis caused by a life of hard labor and carrying heavy loads. After the X-rays, the scientists returned the mummies to their original burial places.

PHARAOHS AND TOMBS

The Pharaoh in Egyptian Art

The Pharaoh was the most powerful person in ancient Egypt. The word Pharaoh means "Great House" and referred to the ruler's palace. One Pharaoh, Pepy II, lived to be 100 years old and ruled for either ninety-four or sixty-four years, depending on which Egyptologist you believe. (In case you're wondering, Pepy II came to the throne when he was six years old!) Other Pharaohs, like King Tut (Tutankhamun), died as teenagers. The Egyptian people believed the Pharaoh was a god on earth.

It was the craftsperson's job to give the Pharaoh an air of strength and authority, to make him look like a god. A Pharaoh's portrait could serve as shelter for his *ka* if anything happened to the mummy. There are three features to look for in a portrait of a Pharaoh: a cobra snake (uraeus) rising from the forehead, a false beard, and a special headdress or crown.

Bronze statuette of kneeling Tutankhamun.

Pharaohs are often shown wearing one of three crowns: the Red Crown of Lower (northern) Egypt, the White Crown of Upper (southern) Egypt, or the Double Crown of a united Upper and Lower Egypt.

Relief of three crowns in a coronation scene.
Left to right: Red Crown of Lower Egypt, Double Crown of Upper and Lower Egypt, White Crown of Upper Egypt.

A Closer Look

- Do you see the black line that represents the chin strap used to attach Mycerinus's false beard?
- Look for the uraeus rearing up from the headdress.
- Find an image of a Pharaoh in your gallery. Is the Pharaoh holding anything? It might be the magic handkerchief, which only the Pharaoh held, or it might be a mace (club).
- Note whether the Pharaoh is sitting or standing. Imitate the pose. Do you feel more powerful?

Mycerinus. This Pharaoh was buried in the third pyramid at Giza. The sculpture, now restored, was found in fragments. It had probably been broken up by treasure seekers.

Snake Talk

Cobras are poisonous snakes. When they are nervous, they flatten long ribs in their neck, making it look as if they are wearing a hood. The cobra shown on the Pharaoh's forehead in Egyptian art is the Egyptian cobra. It has a poisonous bite.

A cobra ready to attack.

A striking image The uraeus, a symbol of royalty, represents the cobra in a posture of attack. Capable of giving a nasty bite, the uraeus protected the Pharaoh from enemies.

BIG WIGS Pharaohs were known to cut their hair short and cover it with a wig. "Upper" and "under" wig makers were in charge of the wigs.

Although as many as four queens ruled Egypt, only two of them are well-known. Some queen-wives, like Akhnaten's wife Nefertiti, became very powerful.

Queen Hatshepsut—A Bearded Queen?

Queen Hatshepsut (1504–1457 BC) ruled Egypt as a Pharaoh. She came to the throne as a regent, or stand-in, for her young nephew, but she ruled for about twenty years. She was called "his highness" and was shown in the Egyptian art of the time wearing the Pharaoh's false beard and short kilt. During her reign, Queen Hatshepsut led an active building campaign. She had a limestone tomb built in Thebes, in Upper (southern) Egypt. Inside there were relief sculptures showing her various accomplishments.

Hatshepsut's tomb. This tomb was cut into towering rock cliffs at Deir el-Bahari in western Thebes.

Cleopatra VII (68–30 BC)

Most people think that Cleopatra was Egyptian, but, in fact, she was Greek. Under Alexander the Great, the Greeks conquered Egypt in 333 BC. When Alexander died, each of his generals took a piece of his empire. Ptolemy II became King of Egypt and founded the Ptolemy (pronounced *tall*-a-mee) dynasty. When she was seventeen, Cleopatra became the last Ptolemy to rule Egypt. According to legend, she poisoned herself to death with a snakebite rather than lose Egypt to Roman conquerors. Seven Cleopatras ruled Egypt, but only the famous one ruled on her own.

Cleopatra coin.

CLEOPATRA EYES

Many museums hold the secret to Cleopatra's striking almond-shaped eyes. Tiny kohl pots used to hold black and green eye makeup, and sticks to apply it are commonly found in tombs.

Non-Royal Egyptian Women

Wealthy Egyptian men usually had one legal wife, "the lady of the house." She helped her husband manage the household. Egyptian wives had the same legal rights as their husbands and could inherit property. Mothers nursed and looked after their children for several years. Some wealthy men kept harems. Women of the harem sang, danced, and performed gymnastics for their master.

At their service Some of the servants a well-to-do Egyptian wife looked after were bakers, "scribes of the sideboard," and "bearers of cool drinks."

Word Wizard

Dynasty The word *dynasty* comes from the Greek word, *dynamis*, which means "force" or "power." A dynasty is a line of rulers, usually from the same family. Other words that are derived from *dynamis* include *dynamite* and *dynamic*.

The ancient Egyptians built pyramids as tombs for Pharaohs of the Old Kingdom (circa 2664–2180 BC). The pyramid was just one part of a large complex that included a temple, a smaller Queen's Pyramid, daughters' tombs, and cemeteries for family and important officials.

Victorian travelers pose in front of the Sphinx and pyramids in 1888.

Who built the pyramids at Giza? A permanent work force of craftspeople and laborers built the pyramids. When the Nile River flooded, farmers who couldn't work their fields were also sent to help out on the pyramids.

GRAVE ROBBERS Treasures buried in some Egyptian tombs made them targets for tomb robbers. Workers could not resist the urge to return to secret gravesites to steal treasures they had seen or heard about. Tomb robbers plundered most of the royal tombs even though the Pharaohs were buried deep in the center of the pyramid in a sealed chamber. Some workers broke into old tombs while they were digging new ones. At one point, tomb robberies were so common that government officials hired tomb guards and moved royal mummies around to keep one step ahead of the robbers. Of the thirty tombs belonging to the Pharaohs of the New Kingdom (ca. 1554–1075 BC), all but two were robbed. During one scandal, even trusted government officials were robbing tombs.

FALSE DOORS

The focal point of an Egyptian tomb was a false door. It was believed that a person's *ka* came through the false door to consume food and drinks left for it in the tomb by relatives and priests. At the top of the false door is a horizontal half-cylinder shape. This may be a symbolic curtain rolled up like a window shade. Next to the door are hieroglyphs that identify the person buried in the tomb and list his or her accomplishments.

False door.

 Did the *ka* really eat the food? Leftovers were probably eaten by priests or given away to the community. Animals enjoyed what remained.

 ## Word Wizard

Pyramid The word *pyramid* was probably coined by Greek travelers. The triangular stone structures may have reminded them of one of their cakes, called *pyramidia*, or "wheaten cake."

? Are there pyramids in other places? There are pyramids in Sudan, south of Egypt. These were built by Nubian kings around 700 BC when they ruled Egypt. In Central America and Mexico, there are hundreds of step-pyramids built between 200 and 800 AD. Closer to home, look for a pyramid on a one-dollar bill.

Striking It Rich

King Tut (Tutankhamun) is famous mostly for what was found in his tomb. It was discovered in 1922 by English archaeologists Howard Carter and the Earl of Carnarvon. Although robbers previously had broken into the tomb, they had left it largely undisturbed. The tomb's contents included boomerangs for hunting, a trumpet, an ostrich feather fan, earrings, rings and necklaces, a lock of his grandmother's hair, a solid gold mask, and almost 100 pairs of shoes. The golden coffin is one of the most celebrated gold objects ever made.

Gold death mask of King Tut. The mask is solid gold and weighs 22.5 pounds. Notice the cobra on his headdress.

ART SCOOP

A mummy's curse? The same day that archaeologist Howard Carter opened King Tut's tomb, Carter's pet canary was eaten by a cobra. Five months later, Lord Carnarvon died suddenly in Egypt. At the time of Carnarvon's death, it was reported that all the lights in Cairo went out. These events started the rumor of a mummy's curse.

An Egyptian sphinx is a mythical creature. It is an image of the Pharaoh's power. It has the body of a lion and the head of a man. Scholars think that the great sphinx that guards the pyramids in Egypt represents Cephren, the Pharaoh who built the second pyramid at Giza.

Did You Know... An Egyptian sphinx is different from a Greek sphinx. The Greek sphinx has the body of a lion, but it has wings and the head of a woman.

A deep sea sphinx? The stone quarry from which the great Giza sphinx is carved was once part of a coral reef at the bottom of the sea. The quarry is about fifty million years old. Archaeologists have found coral prints and shellfish fossils in the Sphinx's stone body. The monument of the sphinx itself, however, is relatively young. It was made only about 4,500 years ago! Today, small animals live inside its huge cracks.

Sphinx at Giza. This sphinx is 240 feet long and 66 feet high, and it once had a temple between its paws.

SCULPTURE

Egyptian craftspeople followed certain rules when making sculptures. Figures generally face forward with one foot in front of the other and their hands at their sides. Sometimes they are seated with their hands on their knees. Important people are larger than the people next to them.

Portrait sculpture served as a substitute home for a person's *ka* if his or her mummy was destroyed. One Egyptian term for a sculptor was "He who makes it live." A portrait sculpture guaranteed that its owner would live happily ever after in the afterlife. It was important that an owner's name was inscribed on the sculpture. Without the subject's name, the sculpture was considered unfinished.

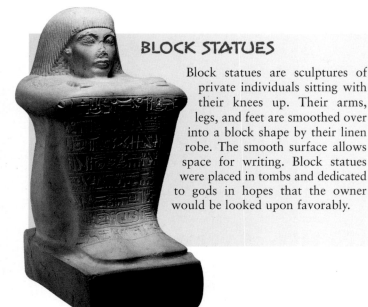

BLOCK STATUES

Block statues are sculptures of private individuals sitting with their knees up. Their arms, legs, and feet are smoothed over into a block shape by their linen robe. The smooth surface allows space for writing. Block statues were placed in tombs and dedicated to gods in hopes that the owner would be looked upon favorably.

Block statue of Ay. Ay was a priest and a relative of the royal family.

What are the round things Egyptians hold in their hands? No one is certain. Archaeologists are still debating the question. They agree that hands grasping something contributes to a solid and permanent look that indicates everlasting life. The knob-like shapes may depict rolls of linen.

Relief Sculpture

A relief sculpture shows a non-freestanding image carved on a stone block. In Egyptian relief sculpture, a person's head, torso, and legs are shown in profile, but the eye is frontal and stares at the viewer. Both shoulders also face the viewer. Relief sculptors combined a profile and frontal eye to give as much information as possible about a person. Often feet are shown only from an inside view, with two big toes and no difference between the left or right foot.

Relief from the Tomb of Akhethotep. This Egyptian official carries a long staff and short sceptre, which are signs of his importance. The hieroglyphs to the right of his face tell his name.

A   Closer Look

• What do you notice about Akhethotep's feet?
• Can you find two inside feet in your gallery?
• While looking at a person's profile, can you find an eye looking straight out at you?

How did the Egyptians make sculptures? Craftspeople used copper chisels and wooden mallets to extract stone from quarries. Some scholars also think that craftspeople bored boles several inches apart and filled them with wet sticks, which swelled in the hot sun and cracked the stone. Early sculptures were carved with metal chisels and wooden mallets. Craftspeople used pounding stones to shape the sculpture. They mixed sand and water to give the stone a high polish. Drills were used for fine details such as inscriptions and eye markings. Teams of craftspeople made large statues.

Family groups and husband-and-wife pairs were sometimes sculpted for a wealthy person's tomb. The men are painted a reddish brown, and the women are painted yellow. Men were painted darker because they worked outside in the hot sun. Men wore linen kilts while women wore white linen shifts. Wives are sometimes shown with a hand around their husband's shoulder. Children are very small compared to adults.

Penmeru and his family.

WHERE DID THEY GET LINEN?

Linen was made from flax which grew along the Nile River. Its strong fibers were woven to make clothes.

- Notice that most Egyptian men stand facing front with their left foot forward, and women tend to stand with their feet together.
- Where is Penmeru's wife's hand? Are there any women with hands around their husband's shoulders in your gallery?
- Look for sculptures or reliefs of Egyptian children. They usually hold a finger up to their lips.
- Can you find some men's kilts and women's shifts?

Why Are Children in Egyptian Art Naked?

Children are shown nude in Egyptian art because they wore no clothes through early childhood. Egypt is a hot country. When you were small, you might have run around naked on a hot day, too! In art, children are shown wearing the "side-lock of youth," a pigtail on one side of their head. The god Horus was said to have worn this hairstyle as a child.

EGYPTIAN CHILDREN Egyptian children liked the same things children do today. Tombs contain spinning tops, balls, toy crocodiles with moving jaws, and dolls with flexible arms and long hair. The young King Tut's burial chamber contained a paint set and a board game called "Snake." Parents sometimes gave their children names that express a thought, such as "Beautiful as her father" or "She is healthy." One Egyptian name, Susan (meaning "lily"), is familiar to us today.

 Why do children hold their fingers up to their mouths? No one knows for sure. Maybe because they are used to saying "Shhh...."

In ancient Egypt, scribes were among the few people (perhaps as few as 1% of the population) who knew how to read and write. They were highly respected and were exempt from manual

Scribe portrait of an unknown man. The scribe is holding a papyrus scroll across his lap and is poised to write.

work and taxes. A scribe recorded wills, taxes, business dealings, and legal disputes. Boys started scribe school between the ages of five and nine. They stayed in school for five years and worked from sunrise until sunset. As part of their training, they copied stories, poems, and letters.

The Write Stuff

In Egyptian sculpture, scribes are shown sitting cross-legged holding a papyrus scroll on their kilt, which served as a lap desk. In wall paintings and relief carvings, scribes sometimes have pens stuck behind their ears. The hieroglyph for scribe shows all the tools of his trade: a reed brush holder, a water bottle, and an ink palette with two holes for red and black ink. It looks like an electrical outlet!

• Can you find a scribe in your gallery? Look at wall reliefs as well as portrait sculpture.

• Look at a scribe's hands. If his palms are up or down, it means he is reading or resting. If his hand looks as if he could hold a pen, he is writing or taking dictation.

• Can you find any pens stuck behind a scribe's ears?

• Look for the hieroglyph for scribe.

What did scribes write on? Student scribes practiced on wood boards covered with plaster or limestone chips found in the desert. These were called *ostracon*. When students became better trained, they wrote on paper, which was made from thinly sliced papyrus stalks that were crisscrossed and pounded with a stone or shell until they formed a smooth sheet.

UTILITY POLES

Papyrus is a tall stalky plant that grew in marshy areas of the Nile River. Marked by a triangular stem, it grew about twelve feet tall and could be as thick as a person's wrist. Apart from paper, papyrus was also used for boats, sails, shoes, and boxes. It is also a decorative motif on furniture, temple columns, and stone reliefs. Can you guess where our word *paper* comes from?

Where did scribes get their ink? Black came from soot and red from a natural earth mixture called *ochre*. These colors were mixed with a gum binder.

Word Wizard

Scribble Can you guess where the word *scribble* comes from? It comes from the Latin verb *scribere,* which means "to write." Now you know where the word *scribe* comes from, too!

Hieroglyphs

Hieroglyphs is the term for the picture writing of the ancient Egyptians. They were first used in Egypt about 5,000 years ago. The pictures and symbols used in hieroglyphic writing can represent both sounds and words. For example, the ear of an ox is the hieroglyph for the word "hear," while the hieroglyph of a "mouth" indicates an "r" sound. Scholars have identified about 700 different hieroglyphic signs.

Do Egyptians use hieroglyphs today?
Hieroglyphs have not been used for about 1,500 years. Arabic is the language written and spoken in Egypt today.

Do you say *hieroglyphs* or *hieroglyphics*?
The word hieroglyph is a noun. You carve hieroglyphs. Hieroglyphic is an adjective. You copy hieroglyphic writing.

What do the hieroglyphs on sculptures say?
Hieroglyphs identify statues and tombs. They tell you a person's name and what he or she did. Sometimes they express magic spells and prayers for the owner.

How did people know where to start reading?
You normally read hieroglyphs in horizontal bands in the direction that animals and people face. They can be read from left to right, or right to left, or even top to bottom in vertical columns.

A   Closer Look

• Can you find hieroglyphs shaped like this?

is the symbol for life.   is the symbol for water.

RATS

A mouth ⬭ is the symbol for the letter "r."

A vulture 𓅐 is the symbol for the letter "a."

A loaf of bread ◠ is the symbol for the letter "t."
Now you can write the word "rat" in hieroglyphs.

What a relief! Sometimes hieroglyphs were formed by gouging out stone to make the symbol or picture. This kind of hieroglyph is called **sunk relief** because the shape sinks into the stone. But sometimes the stone was chipped away from around a symbol, allowing it to rise above the stone surface. This is called **raised relief**. The head of George Washington on the front of a quarter is an example of raised relief.

An example of sunken relief.

A Closer Look

• Look for sunk relief.
• Look for raised relief. Would you write your name faster in sunk relief or raised relief?
• Which style would be better for writing outside? **(answer:** Sunk relief. Shadows inside made them easier to read.)

ART SCOOP

Erasing history Sometimes Egyptian Pharaohs erased the names of earlier rulers from sculptures honoring them. Ramses the Great was famous for removing other Pharaohs's cartouches and reinscribing his own. That is why some of his cartouches are so deep. This habit earned him the name "Ramses the chiseler."

AT HOME IN EGYPT

Little is known about the common people of ancient Egypt. Researchers speculate that many worked from sunup to sundown with the constant supervision of a boss. The only break was when the overseer went for a rest at noon. At the end of the day the workers returned to their small flat-roofed, mud-brick homes. After dinner, they may have played with their children and gone to the village to hear a storyteller. At bedtime, they slept indoors on straw mats, or outdoors on the roof, with the stars as their ceiling. Maybe they dreamed of what they would take with them for their life after death, for they too planned for the afterlife.

Food in Egyptian Art

Barley and emmer wheat formed the backbone of the Egyptian diet. Barley was used to make beer, the most popular drink in ancient Egypt. Emmer wheat was ground into flour to make bread. Most Egyptians ate fish and vegetables such as onions, garlic, beans, and lettuce. They also enjoyed fruits such as dates, figs, and melons. Roast goose was a favorite for special occasions. Wealthy Egyptians ate poultry and beef, and drank wine.

A Closer Look

• Notice how the loaves of bread stand straight up and look like an old-fashioned radiator.

• Find an offering table with bread in your Egyptian collection.

• How many kinds of food do you recognize in a wall painting or relief? You should be able to spot birds, ox legs, bread, figs, or onions.

Stela of Ged-atum-iuf-ankh.

Did You Know...

Open Wide! Archaeologists have found that the teeth of many mummies were worn down by the bread they ate. When the wheat was ground by stone for flour, desert sand and grit sometimes blew in. Archaeologists believe that the course texture of the bread took a toll on teeth.

The ancient Egyptians had more than thirty kinds of bread. Some of it was like our sahara or pita bread. Some museums have displays of bread that is four thousand years old! Look for it and look for the baker's ancient thumbprints.

That's worth beans! Ancient Egyptians used a form of bartering to pay for goods and services. A farmer might pay for cloth with a chicken, but he might pay his taxes in fish, farm produce, animals, or manual labor. Wages were sometimes paid in beans and onions. Scribes kept track of every transaction.

The ancient Egyptians enjoyed entertaining, although it was mostly royalty and high government officials who took part in the most elaborate celebrations. Banquets were given on special occasions, especially for funerals and festivals for the gods. Guests were treated to musicians playing shoulder harps, oboes, and lyre flutes. Love songs were often recited to accompany the orchestra, and dancers added to the festive atmosphere.

A Closer Look

• How many kinds of musical instruments can you find in your Egyptian collection? Look in display cases, as well as on wall paintings and reliefs.
• Can you find a banquet scene, or one showing an orchestra?
• Find a scene of dancers. Try to imitate their poses.

Party time

Servants worked for days to prepare for a banquet. The outdoor fires roasted gazelle, beef, and duck. The bakers' ovens produced sweet cakes and breads with dates or sesame seeds. Tall, slender wine jars were filled with wine made from the host's vineyards. Finally the tables were set with alabaster or glass wine cups and plates made of bronze, pottery, faience, or alabaster. Bowls of water were ready to pour over the guests' sticky fingers since there were no forks.

Party hats

As guests arrived for parties, a fragrant cosmetic cone was placed on their heads. This incense cone, made of perfumed fat, gave off a sweet aroma as it melted down the guest's head and shoulders.

Banquet scene.

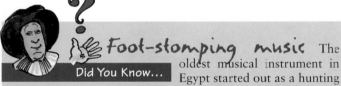

Foot-stomping music The oldest musical instrument in Egypt started out as a hunting tool. Two sticks were clapped together to flush out small game and birds from the Nile marshes. Once the prey was in the open, the sticks were thrown for the kill. Later the sticks took the shape of arms and were used to make music. These clappers were played during grape harvesting to keep time for the stompers crushing the grapes. Clappers were often buried in tombs to scare away evil spirits. Look for a pair of clappers made of ivory or carved on a relief.

CHECKERS, ANYONE?

Ancient Egyptians passed some of their free time playing board games, and were often buried with the games in their tombs. The game of Senet is shown on many wall reliefs and was a particular favorite. Like checkers, senet was played by moving game pieces across a board of marked squares. The first person to remove all of his or her pieces was the winner.

Animals in Egyptian Art

Many tomb carvings show animals—everything from wild animals to exotic foreign animals, to farm animals and family pets. Cattle, donkeys, goats, sheep, and geese were common. Goats and cows were used for milk, which was stored in pottery jugs with grass tops to keep out bugs. Certain wild animals, like crocodiles and hippopotami, were common in ancient Egypt but don't exist there today.

Relief of attendants harpooning hippopotami. These hunters are spearing hippopotami from a papyrus boat in the Nile marshes. Hippopotami were hunted for sport and because they ate farmer's crops.

A Closer Look

- Look for farm animals on Egyptian wall paintings and reliefs.
- Look for different kinds of dogs on tomb paintings and reliefs. Can you tell what type of dogs they are?
- Can you find a cat in your gallery?

Wealthy Egyptians had various pets including dogs, cats, monkeys, hares, and geese, to name a few. The most common pet in ancient Egypt was the dog. One common type resembled the greyhound. Dogs were used for hunting and herding livestock around the fields. Cats were also popular pets. Tomb reliefs show that they were used for retrieving water and ground birds. Some owners even pierced their cat's ears!

Bastet, daughter of the sun god, was a cat goddess whose cult center was in the delta. She is associated with the sistrum, a sacred rattle. Thousands of cat mummies and numerous bronze cat figures were made in her honor.

Bronze cat. This cat is wearing a gold hoop earring.

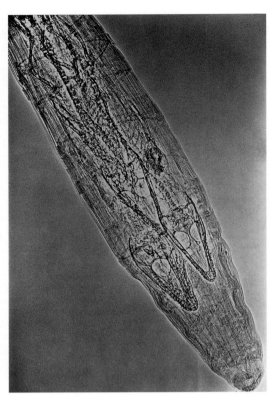

Crocodile mummy X-ray.

Even crocodiles! There are no wild crocodiles in Egypt now, but in ancient times they were common. When the Greeks colonized ancient Egypt, they named a city after the god Sobek, who took the form of a crocodile. They called it Crocodilopolis. Priests in Crocodilopolis kept a pool full of bejeweled crocodiles sacred to Sobek. When the crocodiles died, they were mummified.

Did You Know... Egyptian children were sometimes named after animals. Frog, Mouse, Monkey, Wolf, and Hippopotamus are but a few recorded examples!

Pet Lions and War?

Ramses II had a pet lion that went into battle with him and slept outside his tent!

CAMEL TALK

Camels were not used for transportation in Egypt until about 2,000 years after the Great Pyramids were built. Until then, donkeys were the main means of getting around. Scientists believe that the first camels actually lived in North America 175,000 years ago. In the 1850s, the U.S. army briefly used camels to transport supplies from Texas to California.

Why do camels make faces? Camels are known to be cranky. They grunt and groan and make faces. Legend says there is a reason for this. The prophet Mohammed told the secret-of-all-secrets, the 100th name of Allah, to the camel. Each camel passed it on to another camel. When a camel sees a person who doesn't know the 100th name of Allah, he makes a face of disgust.

An Arabian camel. The Arabian camels seen in Egypt have one hump. Bactrian, or two-humped camels, live in Asia.

Jewelry

In ancient Egypt, wealthy men and women wore jewelry. Both men and women wore necklaces, upper arm and wrist bracelets, anklets, and earrings. Common jewelry motifs were animals, gods, lucky symbols such as the ankh and scarab beetle, and the lotus.

Colors with clout Sometimes gemstone colors had special meanings. **Blue**, made with rare lapis lazuli, might suggest the gods. **Green** might suggest growth and fertility. **Red** symbolized life blood, and **gold** stood for the sun.

Sun Flower The lotus is a lily that grows in the Nile River. Because its petals closed at night and opened in the morning, it became a symbol of rebirth. An Egyptian creation myth says that Ra, the sun god, entered the world on the petals of a lotus.

HEAVY METAL The most common piece of jewelry worn by men and women was the broad-collar necklace known as the *wesekh,* which means "the broad one."

These heavy looking necklaces were made of gold or *faience,* a glassy paste baked in a mold. It was made by craftspeople from crushed quartz paste and colored pigments. Faience is usually turquoise or blue but can also be yellow, red, or green.

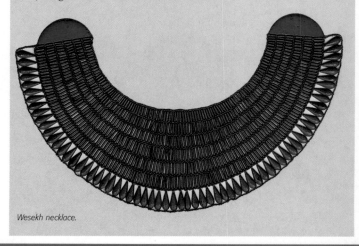

Wesekh necklace.

Amulets are good luck charms. People wore them on bracelets and necklaces. The Egyptians also put amulets into mummy wrappings for good luck. Children sometimes wore fish amulets in their hair—maybe to protect them from falling into the Nile River.

Hedgehogs The lowly hedgehog appears sometimes on tomb reliefs and paintings. The Egyptians may have viewed the hedgehog as a symbol of courage because of its habit of curling up into a ball and showing its spines to an attacker.

Hedgehog amulet. A medical papyrus suggests that hedgehogs' spines were ground up with oil to help cure baldness.

• Look for broad-collar necklaces, bracelets, and anklets painted on sculptures of Egyptian men and women.

• Look for amulets. Can you find an ankh, an eye of Horus, and a scarab?

A   Closer Look

• Look for necklaces made of a single strand of beads. These were the oldest types of jewelry worn in ancient Egypt. They were made of shell, copper, faience, and gold.

• Look for earrings worn by government officials, women, and children. Notice the different styles: hoops, studs, plugs, and dangles.

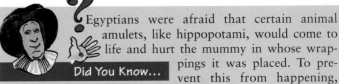

Egyptians were afraid that certain animal amulets, like hippopotami, would come to life and hurt the mummy in whose wrappings it was placed. To prevent this from happening, they broke the legs of the amulet. Only then was it safe to put into the mummy's wrappings. Snakes were sometimes painted on coffins in two separate pieces for the same reason.

Silver More Valuable Than Gold?

For a long time, silver was considered more precious than gold in ancient Egypt because it was rarer. Gold was plentiful in Nubia to the south, but sometimes the intense heat made it hard to get to. On some mining expeditions, half the miners died of dehydration.

*Funerary stele of Amen-em-hab.
Goldsmiths made jewelry as well as
the gold lining of King Tut's coffin.*

A Closer Look

• What are the goldsmith and his wife facing? (**answer:** an offering table piled high with food for the next life)

• Compare the feet of the chair with the people's feet. What similarities do you notice? What differences?

• Look in your gallery for an example of sunk or raised relief. Check for the following: an offering table, a chair, the eyes of Horus, and hieroglyphs.

Cosmetic Palettes and Makeup

You can take it with you! The Egyptians believed they could take their things with them to the afterlife. Their graves are full of everyday necessities. Many objects for grooming have been found buried in tombs. Some include bronze razors, tweezers, mirrors, and wooden combs. The ancient Egyptians were very concerned about their appearance, even in the afterlife! Cosmetic palettes, which were used to grind eye makeup, are also commonly found in Egyptian graves. The palettes were often shaped like animals and fish. Both men and women wore eye makeup made out of malachite, a mineral made from copper, and kohl, a lead ore. They probably drew lines above and below their eyes to protect themselves from the sun and to ward off flies. Chances are they liked the way it made them look, too!

Cosmetic palettes.

• Find two cosmetic palettes in your museum. How are they shaped?

• Can you find traces of ancient green eye makeup in the middle of a cosmetic palette?

A Closer Look

• Can you locate a shiny grinding stone in the case?

TACKLING EYE MAKEUP

Who puts black under their eyes for protection from the sun today?

(**answer:** football players)

From Head to Toe

The leaves and roots of the Egyptian privet bush were ground into an orange-red paste called henna. In addition to fingernail and toenail paint, it was used to color the beards of men and the manes of horses. For special occasions, horses' hooves were also colored with henna.

Wigging Out

Pharaohs weren't the only Egyptians to wear wigs. It was the custom for wealthy men and women to cut their hair short and wear wigs also. Wigs were made from human hair or sheep's wool. Braids of wig hair were threaded through gold tubes. The tiny beaded decoration on the tubes was repeated on earrings and bracelets, creating a matching set of jewelry.

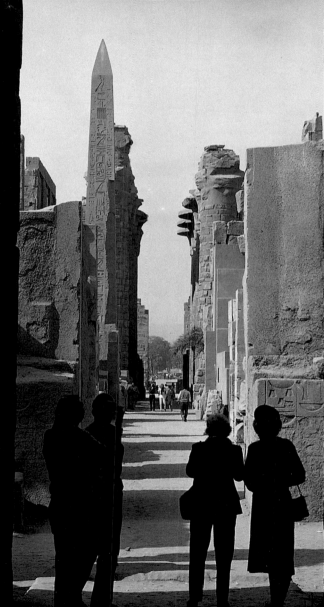

The Myth of Set and Osiris

Osiris was an ancient fertility god of Egypt. His brother, Set, was the god of storms. Set was jealous of Osiris because he was more popular than Set. So Set plotted to kill Osiris. One night he invited Osiris to a banquet. At the end of the evening, Set invited each guest to lie inside a beautiful golden chest. The person who fit best inside the chest could keep it. Each guest hoped to be the lucky one. Nobody knew that Set had secretly measured Osiris in his sleep and had made the chest to fit Osiris. When Osiris lay in the chest, he fit perfectly. Set slammed down the cover, nailed it shut, and threw it into the Nile River.

The chest drifted to Lebanon where a queen found it and used it to repair a palace column. It wasn't long before Isis, a goddess of magic and the wife of Osiris, learned where he was and flew around the palace column in the form of a bird. Isis used her magic to help Osiris escape, but Set found him and chopped him up into thousands of pieces. Isis and her sister pieced Osiris together, and he became Lord of the Underworld. Later, Osiris's son, Horus, fought Set for the kingship of Egypt and defeated him.

Horus, a son of Osiris, was a sun god with the body of a man and the head of a falcon. Sometimes he is shown only as a falcon.

INSIDE LOOKING OUT

The **wedjet eye** is a symbol of completeness. It combines a human eye with the striped markings of a falcon. It represents the eye of Horus which was torn out by his uncle Set in their battle to rule Egypt. Two wedjet eyes frequently appear on coffins where they allow the mummy to look outside on its way to the afterlife. The eye also had the power to protect the mummy inside.

Osiris is the god of the afterlife and father of Horus. In sculpture, he is often shown as a mummy with crossed arms holding a crook and a flail, a manual threshing tool. His face is either a dark green or earth color, pointing to his origin as a god of agriculture.

Bronze statuette of Osiris.

The Sun God's Scary Boat Trip

Ra was the sun god on whom ancient Egyptians depended to cast light on the earth. Day after day, Ra had to fight for his life. Each morning he woke up and took a bath in the Sea of Heaven. Then he got into his shiny sun boat, ready for his all-day sail across the sky. Hour after hour, his people watched his shiny boat move steadily from east to west. When night approached, Ra steered his boat below the western horizon. It was here that Ra entered the Underworld to face a terrible enemy.

The serpent monster Apep hid in the darkness, waiting for Ra. Apep ate no food, for he lived off the vapors from his own hideous howls. But night after night, he hoped to swallow up Ra and his shiny boat. Ra fought Apep in a grisly battle and forced him back into darkness for another day. Out of danger, Ra floated by the caves and coffins of each Underworld god. As he cast his brilliant light on each coffin, he brought each god back to life for a second. At last, safely through the Underworld, Ra returned to the eastern skies, where he could rest before starting his journey again the next morning.

A   Closer Look

- Can you find images of Ra in an Egyptian collection? Look for Ra in his boat.
- Does your collection have a wooden model of a boat?

Ra in his shiny boat. Ra is the father of the gods as well as the sun god. As the sun, Ra rises in the East and disappears below the western horizon at night to do battle with the monster serpent of the Underworld. Ra is shown as a man with a falcon's head wearing a sun disk and uraeus. He is sometimes shown in his little boat crossing the sky.

The Egyptian sun god Ra was depressed. He was old, and the Egyptians were ignoring him. So he asked his daughter, Sekhmet, the lion-headed goddess, to go down to Egypt and scold them. Sekhmet sneaked down to Egypt, but instead of scolding the Egyptian people, she gobbled them up, one by one. Ra begged her to stop. He said, "There will be no one left in Egypt to worship me if you eat them all up." But Sekhmet would not listen. Day after day she feasted on more Egyptians.

Ra had to think of something to stop Sekhmet. One night he filled all the rivers and lakes in Egypt with a mixture of beer and red clay. The next morning, when Sekhmet left her lair, she sniffed a lovely smell. Passing by a lake to admire her reflection, she smelled it again. She lapped a little lake water, and it was delicious. She drank until the lake was drained, and she couldn't move. Sekhmet was drunk! Ra's trick to make her stop eating the Egyptian people had worked. She was never a problem to Ra again.

A Closer Look • Find a statue of Sekhmet. What parts look "lion-ish?" How did the sculptor make her whiskers? Would her ears be up or down if she were angry? Is she holding an ankh?

Standing bronze statuette of Sekhmet. Sekhmet is the lion-headed goddess of war. Associated with fire, she kept order in the universe. She holds an ankh, the Egyptian hieroglyph for life.

Life in their hands The **ankh** is the Egyptian hieroglyph for life. Only gods, goddesses, kings and queens hold it, maybe to show that they could give or take away life.

ACTIVITIES

Hunts

Animal hunt Look for birds, jackals, cats, farm animals, hippos, crocodiles, and lions.

Monster hunt Look for a sphinx, a creature with a human head and a lion's body. Look for Ammit in the Weighing of the Heart scene.

Postcard hunt Find a postcard of an Egyptian object in the museum shop and look for it in the collection.

Hieroglyph hunt Find hieroglyphs for water, the letter "t," and an "r" sound.

Musical hunt Find instruments played in ancient Egypt such as the oboe, shoulder harp, lyre, and clappers (like castanets).

Traces-of-paint hunt Look for evidence of paint on sculptures.

Fish hunt Find three different fish. Fish were sometimes used to pay taxes.

Just-got-out-of-bed hunt Find cases containing a mirror, razor, tweezers, combs, hairpins, and a tiny vial for eye makeup called a kohl pot, or any other domestic items used in a typical day in ancient Egypt.

Foot hunt See how many "funny" or "same" feet you can find.

Games

Theme tours Take a day trip to ancient Egypt. Set out by saying, "Let's take a boat trip down the Nile River in Egypt and see what we can find."

Memory game You and a friend choose a work of art. Both of you study it for several minutes. Turn away from the object and see how many things you can remember about what you saw. Who remembers the most?

Role playing Find two people in a relief carving. Make up a conversation between them. Act it out with a friend.

Mnemonics

Mnemonics (pronounced na-*mon*-icks) are word tricks used to help remember important things. Words and letters can jog your memory. You can use mnemonics to remember highlights of a museum visit.

As you look at a work of art, play with **MUD**.

M   **Materials** What material is it made of? Is it stone, wood, alabaster, bronze?
U   **Use** What do you think the object was used for? For the tomb? For pleasure? For the house? For worship?
D   **Design or decoration** Is the object brightly painted or plain? Is the design carved or added on? If you took away the design or decoration, how would it change the look and feel of the object?

ILLS Find four animal-headed canopic jars. Remember what went inside—Intestines, Lungs, Liver, Stomach.

Intestines	Falcon head
Lungs	Baboon head
Liver	Human head
Stomach	Jackal head

Making Art

- Draw the outline of a mummy and decorate it.
- Sketch something you want to take home.
- Use a shoebox as a tomb chamber. Instead of decorating it with the things you would take with you to the next world, draw what you would take with you on a long car trip.
- Draw your own amulet or good luck charm. Then thread a shoelace through it to make a necklace.
- Find some tube pasta. Paint it blue and gold and put it on a single or double string. You have made an Egyptian necklace!

Mad Lib

Sekhmet, the Lion-Headed Goddess, Visits the Doctor

Once upon a time, the lion-headed goddess, Sekhmet, was feeling sick, so she made an appointment with Dr. (name) _____. "My, you look rather (color) _____ and sickly," the doctor said when he saw her. "Let's have a look at your (word that comes to mind after looking at an object for a long time) _____ ears. Ah, yes, very droopy—a bad symptom in a lion."

The doctor put his hand on her (word that comes to mind after looking hard at an object) _____ forehead and told her that she had a temperature of (number) _____ degrees! Then he peered into her (word that comes to mind after looking at an object for a long time) _____ eyes and up her (word which comes to mind after looking hard at an object) _____ nose and felt her (word which comes to mind after looking hard at an object) _____ whiskers. "Now say (noise) _____," he added, looking in her mouth.

Next he poked her tummy. "H'mm, what have you been eating? Too many honey cakes, stewed figs, and (a kind of food) _____, I suspect. Here is a prescription for honey and lizard blood. You will feel better in (number) ___ days. Meanwhile, it isn't wise to wear your (word that comes to mind after looking hard at an object) _____ wig or lift your (word that comes to mind after looking hard at an object) _____ ankh with such a high fever."

Recipes

Make Pharaoh's favorite breakfast bread or some Pyramid (pita bread) triangles, Egyptian-style.

Pharaoh's Favorite Breakfast Bread
Blend 2 cups of whole wheat flour with ¼ teaspoon of salt and 1 cup of warm water. Knead well. Shape any way you want. Decorate with thumb presses, Egyptian-style. Bake for ½ hour at 350 degrees. This makes a small amount.

Pyramid Bread Triangles
Buy a package of pita bread. Cut it into pyramid shapes (triangles) and toast it. Pretend you are the Pharaoh and put whatever you want on it.